LITTLEPORT CO

Origin
Fee Fie Fo ... Mum!

Sîan Lewis Garry Parsons

OXFORD
UNIVERSITY PRESS

Chapter 1 – Terrible twins

Sam and Samantha were nine-year-old twins.
They looked alike.
They sounded alike.
They were always arguing.

One Saturday morning Mum was making breakfast.

It was a fine sunny day. The birds were singing. The bees were humming. Dad was whistling an out-of-tune tune.

"Breakfast!" called Mum.

From upstairs came a bang, a screech and a yell. The birds flew away in fright. The bees stopped humming. Dad put his fingers in his ears.

"Oh, no," sighed Mum. "Those two are trying to race each other again."

The twins ran along the hall and tried to squeeze through the door.

"Get out of my way!" shrieked Samantha.

"Stop pushing me!" yelled Sam.

"Ouch!" They both crashed into the kitchen table.

SLOP! went the milk.

PITTER PATTER! went the cornflakes.

CLANG! went the spoons.

Sam snatched up the egg in the blue egg cup.

"Careful!" wailed Mum, diving to catch the plate just in time.

"Sam's taken the blue egg cup!" yelled Samantha. "It's mine!"

"It's not!" yelled Sam.

Smash! went the egg.

Smash!

"Stop it!" roared Mum. "It's not funny." She picked up the phone and dialled a number. "Hello," she said. "Is that the Youth Centre?"

"Yes," said a voice. "Darren speaking. How can I …?" Darren held the phone away from his ear and gasped at the noise.

"Hello! Have you any classes for nine-year-olds on a Saturday morning?" shouted Mum.

"There's a drama workshop starting in ten minutes," Darren shouted back.

"Thank you," said Mum. "I'll bring Sam and Samantha along."

Mum put the phone down, snatched up a piece of paper and wrote:

You two are going to drama class.

Now!

Then she waved the paper in front of her noisy twins and shooed them out to the car.

Chapter 2 – Meet the Cast

Mum stopped outside the Youth Centre.

"Ooh, look at that poster!" she said. "The Young Drama Group is putting on a *Jack and the Beanstalk* show."

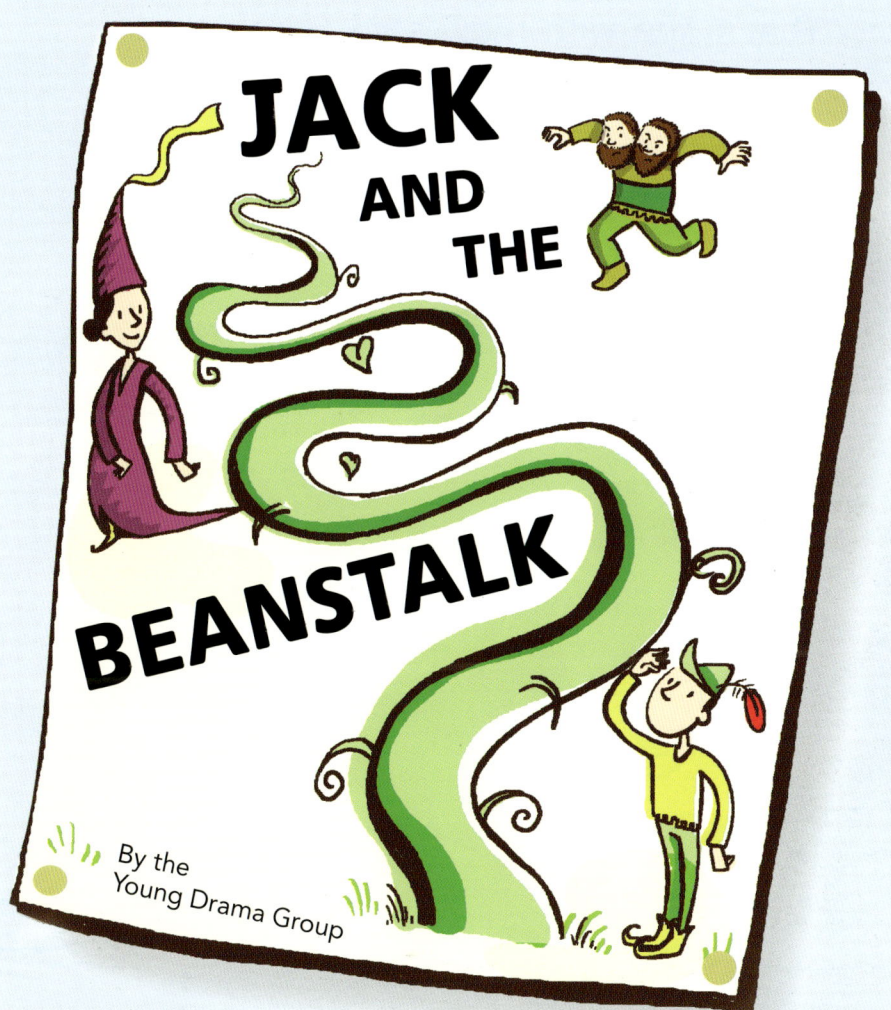

JACK AND THE BEANSTALK

By the Young Drama Group

"Isn't that exciting?" said Mum.

"No," said Sam.

"It might be," said Samantha. "I wouldn't mind being that princess on the poster."

"In your dreams!" sneered Sam.

"Now don't argue," said Mum anxiously. "Keep well away from each other."

"That's fine with me," said Samantha, scowling at her brother.

Just then, a cheerful young man put his head round the door. He smiled at the twins.

"Hi, you must be Sam and Samantha. And you're twins! That's great!" he called. "I'm Darren, the director. Come and meet the team."

"Hello, Darren," said Samantha in the sort of voice a princess might use.

She ducked under his arm and stepped into the hall, where a harp plink-plonked.

"That's Katy who plays the harp – and *plays* the harp!" said Darren.

Samantha blinked. Katy wasn't just *playing* a harp. She was dressed like a harp too.

"Hello-o," sang Katy.

"Hello!" called the other members of the drama group.

Sam and Samantha's heads swivelled around like spy cameras. The place was a beehive of activity. There were people painting scenery, people sewing costumes and people setting up lights. Everybody had a role, not just the actors.

And Katy wasn't the only one who was wearing a costume. Brad was waddling around dressed as a goose. Ellie was having an enormous apron pinned up so she didn't trip on it, while Josh was wearing a green tunic over his jeans and pretending to fight his reflection in the mirror.

But who was wearing the princess dress? No one!

The princess dress was lying on the stage on top of a hairy, old rug. Samantha grinned to herself.

Chapter 3 – The big hairy giant

Brad the Goose waddled up to Samantha with two sheets of paper in his beak.

"Honk! Honk! Here's a bit of the script for you to try out," he said.

"Thank you," said Samantha.

Scene 6
In the giant's Castle

Giant: Fee Fie Fo Fum! I smell a nasty smell. How come?

Harp: It's Jack!

Goose: He's stolen my golden egg

Harp: And I think he's stolen Princess Meg!

Giant: He won't get far. I'll squash him flat. And then I'll feed him to the cat.

Samantha read the first page very carefully. Then she read the second page. On both pages there were speeches for the Goose, the Harp and the Giant but none at all for Princess Meg. The Harp was Katy and the Goose was Brad. That left ...

"Uh-oh!" whispered Samantha. Her grin disappeared. She looked across at Sam. Sam was reading the same two pages of the script. "Uh-oh" whispered Samantha again, as a horrible thought crossed her mind. Her face began to wobble and her tummy began to feel a bit odd.

"OK?" called Darren cheerfully. "Ready to try out your part? I expect you've guessed by now that we're doing the story of *Jack and the Beanstalk*. We've written the words ourselves but we can change them as we go along."

Samantha said nothing. She was watching Aisha put on the princess dress. That made her tummy feel odder still.

Then Aisha reached for the mothy old rug.
"Do you want to try this on?" she called.

Samantha gulped. The rug wasn't really a rug at all. It was an enormous giant's costume with hairy arms and a baggy old tunic that reached down to the floor.

"Yes, come on," said Darren. He shooed Sam and Samantha forward and helped Aisha pull the hairy old costume over their heads.

Chapter 4 – Two heads are better than one

Sam's head popped out of the top of the giant's costume. Samantha's head popped up beside him.

"Yuck!" gasped Sam. "What are you doing here?"

"Yuck yourself," said Samantha.

BUMP! went their noses.

"Get out of my costume!" hissed Sam.

"It's my costume too," said Samantha.

"Don't be silly," snapped Sam. "We can't both be the giant at the same time."

"Yes, we can," said Samantha, pointing at the mirror.

Sam nearly jumped out of his hairy skin. In the mirror a monster with two heads was scowling at him.

"A two-headed giant!" he gasped. "No way! I don't want to be stuck with you."

In a panic Sam tried to pull the costume over his head.

"Stop it! You're pulling me too," squealed Samantha. She stumbled over Sam's feet and they both fell in a heap against Katy's chair.

"Eeeeek!" cried Katy and before the giant could stop her, her chair went whizzing across the room.

> Honk! Honk! Hooray!

The giant's two faces turned bright red.

"Sorry, Katy!" they both cried. "We're very, very sorry!"

"You don't have to be!" said Katy, whizzing back. She was grinning from ear to ear. "That was really funny."

"Really, really funny," said Josh.

"Three cheers for our giant. Honk! Honk! Hooray!" said the Goose.

"We never thought of having a giant with two *quarrelling* heads before," said Aisha excitedly.

"Let's add some quarrelling bits to our play," said Katy.

"Yes!" said the rest of the team.

Katy fished out a pen and a sheet of paper from the side of her chair. Sam and Samantha watched as everyone gathered round her to change the script.

"Hey, come on, you two," Josh called to them.

"You are going to join in, aren't you?" said Ellie.

The two heads of the giant turned to each other.

"Are you?" growled one.

"Try and stop me!" grinned the other.

BUMP! went their noses.

Chapter 5 – Team work

Back home, Sam and Samantha's mum and dad had had a peaceful morning. Now it was time to fetch the twins.

Mum parked behind the Youth Centre. The back door was open and she could hear the children acting. She listened.

"Fee Fie Fo Fum! Let's catch Jack!"

"Sounds exciting!" thought Mum. Then her face turned pale.

"Let's go this way!" yelled a familiar voice.

"No, this way!" yelled another.

"Stop pulling!"

"Stop pushing!"

"Take your horrible nose out of my ear."

"Ouch! You're pinching me."

"Oh, no!" gasped Mum. She rushed through the back door and ran up the stairs.

"Sam! Samantha! Please stop quarrelling!" Mum yelled. "It's not funny!"

"Fee Fie Fo …. MUM!" gasped the giant, as a furious Mum ran onto the stage.

The stage went silent.

Mum turned round, and nearly jumped out of her skin. There behind her stood a hairy monster.

The monster had two heads. One was Sam's and the other was Samantha's. Both heads were looking at her very, very sternly.

"Fee Fie Fo Fum," growled the head on the right.

"What shall we do with the noisy Mum?" said the head on the left.

"Oops!" said Mum, blushing. "Sorry. I thought you were arguing."

"Us?" said Sam and Samantha. "We never argue. We're a team!"

"Yes, they're a team within our team," laughed Darren. "And they are very, very funny!"